"Doodlemaster" ROCK STAR!

BY
Maria S. Barbo

ILLUSTRATED BY
Chuck Gonzales

FEIWEL AND FRIENDS

NEW YORK

A FEIWEL AND FRIENDS BOOK

An Imprint of Macmillan

Printed in September 2009 in the United States of America by
R.R. Donnelley & Sons Company, Willard, Ohio. For information, address
Feiwel and Friends, 175 Fifth Avenue, New York, N.Y. 10010.

Library of Congress Cataloging-in-Publication Data Available

ISBN: 978-0-312-59606-4

Book design by Kathleen Breitenfeld

Feiwel and Friends logo designed by Filomena Tuosto

First Edition: 2009

10 9 8 7 6 5 4 3 2 1

www.feiwelandfriends.com

DON'T YOU DARE TOUCH THIS BOOK!

How are you going to defend the secrets kept in this book?
Draw your warning sign below.

SEE A BLANK SPACE?
DOODLE IN IT!
THIS IS YOUR BOOK.
MAKE IT AS COOL
AS YOU WANT.

Doodlemaster

SCRIBBLE-MANIA

Warm up that drawing
arm by scribbling here:
thin lines, thick lines,
dark lines, light lines,
squares, circles, squiggles,
and made-up shapes.

Now, go back and connect some of the
lines and shapes of your scribbles to
create a brand-new work of art!

AUTOGRAPH SESSION

HEY THERE, ROCK STAR!

You have so many adoring fans. Practice your signature here:

ROCK ON!

You've just been inducted into the Rock and Roll Hall of Fame!
Draw yourself rocking out in front of millions of screaming fans.

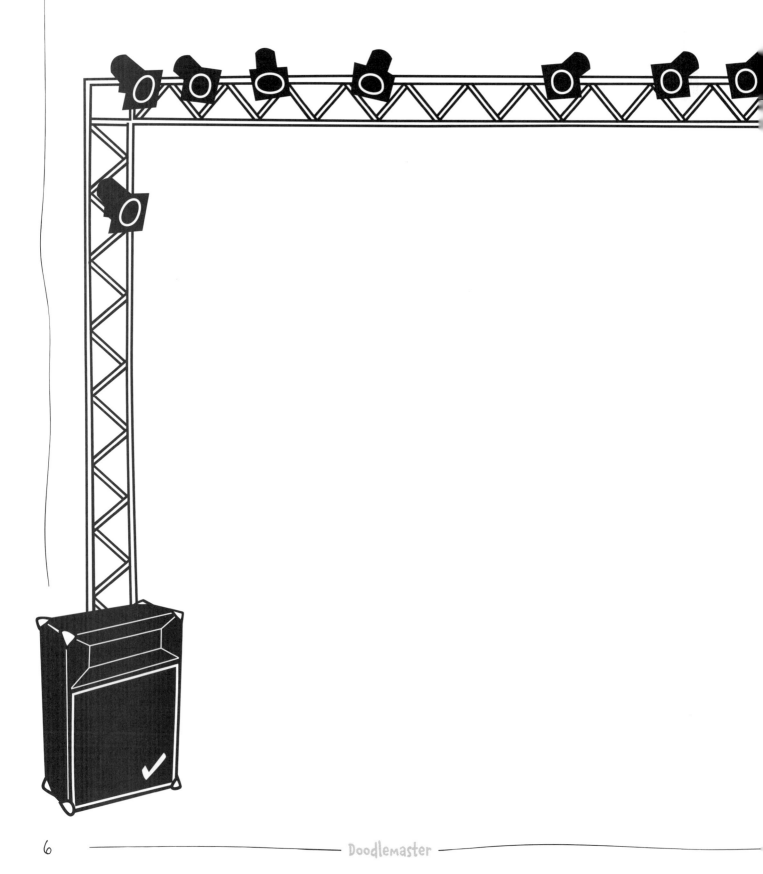

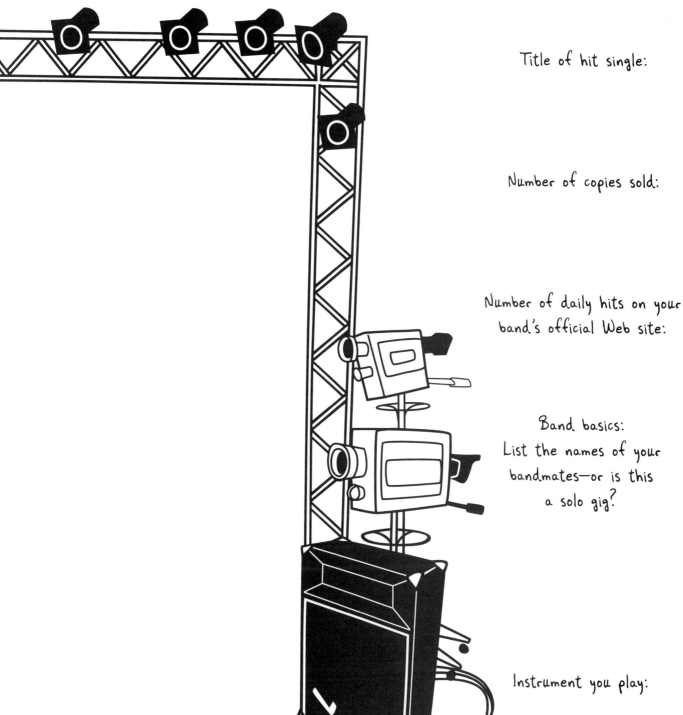

FILL-INS:

Name of your top album:

Title of hit single:

Number of copies sold:

Number of daily hits on your band's official Web site:

Band basics:
List the names of your bandmates—or is this a solo gig?

Instrument you play:

And the winner is...
Congratulations! You just won a KIDS' CHOICE AWARD!
Quick, make your speech before you get slimed!

HAH! TOO SLOW. YOU GOT SLIMED!

MY SPEECH

FILL-INS:

What gets your vote for...

...best movie?

...best actor?

...best actress?

Book you'd most like to
see turned into a movie:

Video game you'd most like to
see turned into a movie:

Book, video game, or toy you hope they
NEVER turn into a movie:

SAVE THE WORLD!

You've only got four minutes to save the world!
How would you stop this?

GROSS-OUT!

Draw your own collection of the grossest items ever:

Things that ooze

Eyeballs

Things that stink

Things that bite

CAR COLLECTION

Rock stars have rockin' cars. Draw your car collection here:

MR. PRESIDENT

From rock star to president of the United States. Sweet!
Congratulations on winning that election, Mr. President.

What's your first order of business?

Now, draw yourself inside Air Force One.

I'd refuse to fly without: Movies we'd watch on board:

Every president needs a new pet.
Draw yours here, and write his/her name.

Doodlemaster

The issue I won my campaign on:

My top three goals for the first 100 days:

My campaign button:

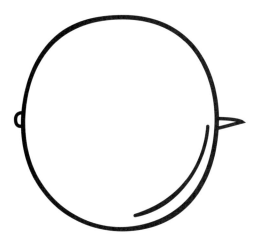

Three things about the country I'd fix right away:

Long-term goal:

BA-ROCK THE WHITE HOUSE!

President Barack Obama turned the presidential bowling alley into a basketball court. Draw your brand-new White House Rec Room here:

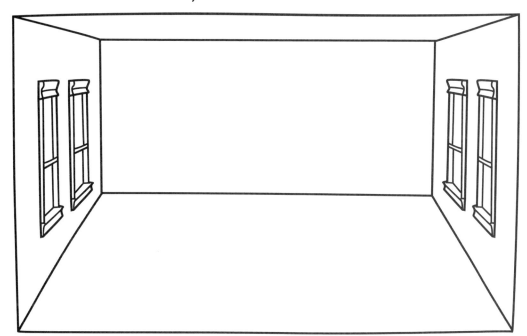

What other changes would you make?

Who would be on your Secret Service team?

ALL ABOUT ME!

CIRCLE YOUR FAVE CHOICES BELOW:

Laptop or desktop?

PC or Mac?

Breakfast or lunch?

Chips or pizza?

Soda or juice?

Video games or sports?

Sports or books?

Righty or lefty?

Art or music?

Rock Band or Guitar Hero?

Guitar or drums?

Hanging out or going out?

Mashed potatoes or French fries?

Fried chicken or tacos?

Early bird or night owl?

Skateboard or bike?

Baseball or football?

Basketball or soccer?

Doodlemaster

READY, SET, GO!

Draw your ultimate race car.

ZOMBIES ATTACK!

How would you and your bandmates get out of this scary situation?

Doodlemaster

DESIGN YOUR OWN GRAPHIC NOVEL

The story is started—how will it end?

Doodlemaster

TIME TRAVEL

YOU'VE JUST DISCOVERED THE SECRET TO TIME TRAVEL. COOL!

Some physicists believe traveling to the future is possible, so long as you have a vehicle that can move at the speed of light. Draw your design for a turbo-charged time travel machine here. Full speed ahead!

The moment I'd most like to skip ahead to is:

That's so warped! It's much more complicated to travel back in time,
but that doesn't mean you won't figure it out one day. What are the top three
moments you'd most like to go back in time to see? Write or draw them below.

WRESTLEMASTER

Draw yourself in the ring delivering your signature move.

What is your wrestler name?

What is your signature move?

Who are you wrestling?

What is your theme song?

Doodlemaster

HOT DOG-EATING CONTEST

Draw yourself winning a hot dog-eating contest.

MORE ABOUT ME

(Draw or write your answers.)

The funniest thing I ever saw:

If I couldn't watch TV, play video games, or have any screen time for an entire weekend, here are three things I'd do:

1.   2.   3.

My biggest fear (assuming there's something I'm afraid of):

The one thing I'd never do in public:

The dumbest thing I ever did on the playground:

The ugliest shirt my parents ever forced me to wear:

If I could have a lifetime supply of any one food, it would be:

Best ice cream sundae ever created:

AND THE WINNER IS . . .

You just won a million, bajillion dollars! Draw the first three things you'd buy below:

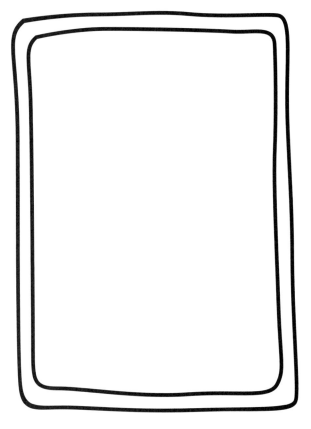

Now, draw a super safe
to protect your bajillions!

Now, draw three ways you'd spend some of your money to help others:

TRANSFORMATIONS

Turn this regular kid into a...

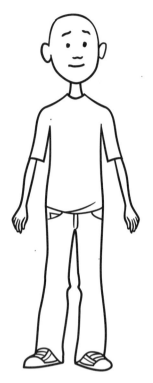

Skater dude

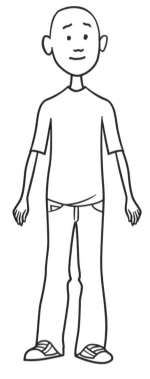

Computer whiz

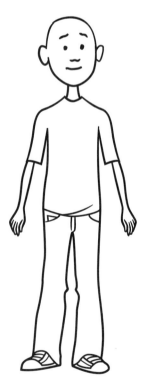

Werewolf

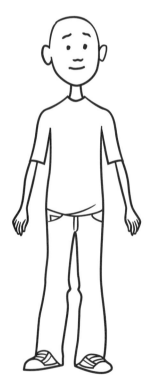

Punk rocker

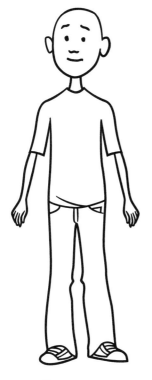

Astronaut

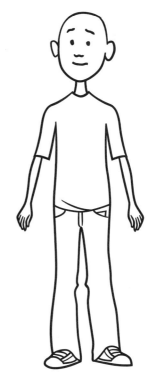

Baseball star

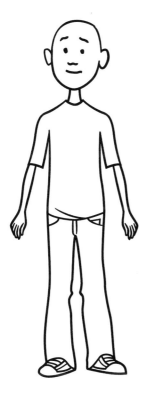

Kung Fu master

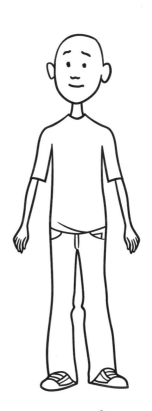

Top chef

DR. DOODLEMASTER

Draw and list your injuries and how you suspect you got them:

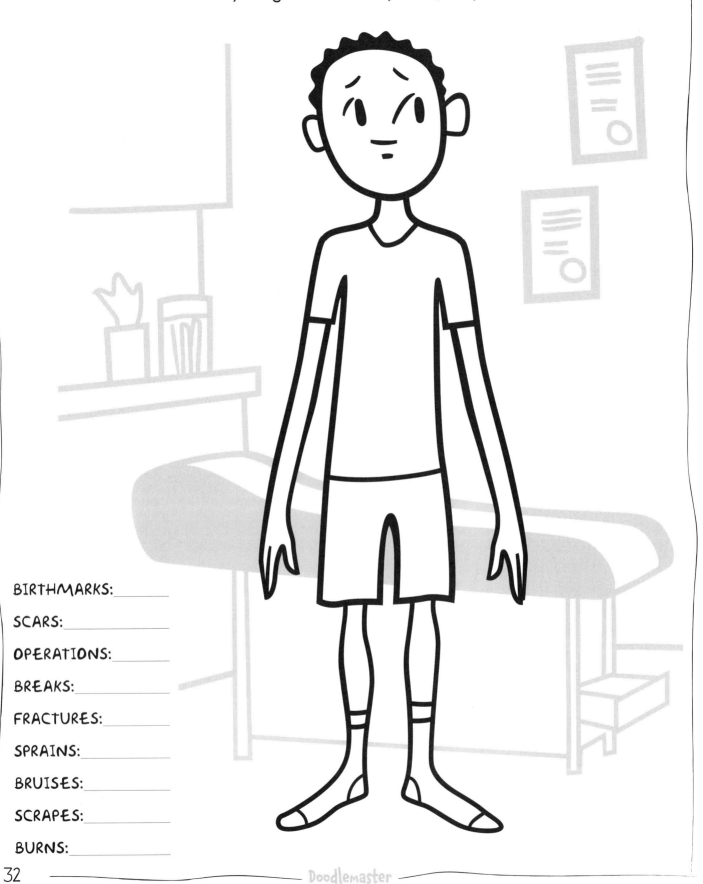

BIRTHMARKS:_____

SCARS:_____

OPERATIONS:_____

BREAKS:_____

FRACTURES:_____

SPRAINS:_____

BRUISES:_____

SCRAPES:_____

BURNS:_____

MYSTERY DOOR

WHAT'S BEHIND THIS DOOR?

SUPERHERO SUPERPOWER

Design for my supersuit:

My top three superpowers are:

1.

2.

3.

My archenemy is:

Even a superhero needs a set of wheels (or wings).
Here's the design for my super-powered supervehicle:

When I'm not fighting crime,
I look like this:

SUPER BOWL HALFTIME

Draw you and your band playing the halftime show at the Super Bowl.

Doodlemaster

Name one person you secretly wish is in the audience:

Name the people you want to be watching from home:

Fave football team(s):

Fave player:

Best football game I've ever seen:

Would you rather get tackled by Dracula or a lunch lady?

Dream team: Who's on it?

BATTLE STATIONS
IN A BATTLE BETWEEN THE FOLLOWING, WHO WOULD WIN?

(Circle your answers and doodle below!)

Vampire vs. Werewolf

Giant Spider vs. Sabertooth Tiger

Giant Octopus vs. Great White Shark

King Kong vs. a Pterodactyl

Pirates vs. Vikings

Zombie vs. Mummy

Alien Army vs. Swarm of Giant Bees

Who's battling in the arena below?

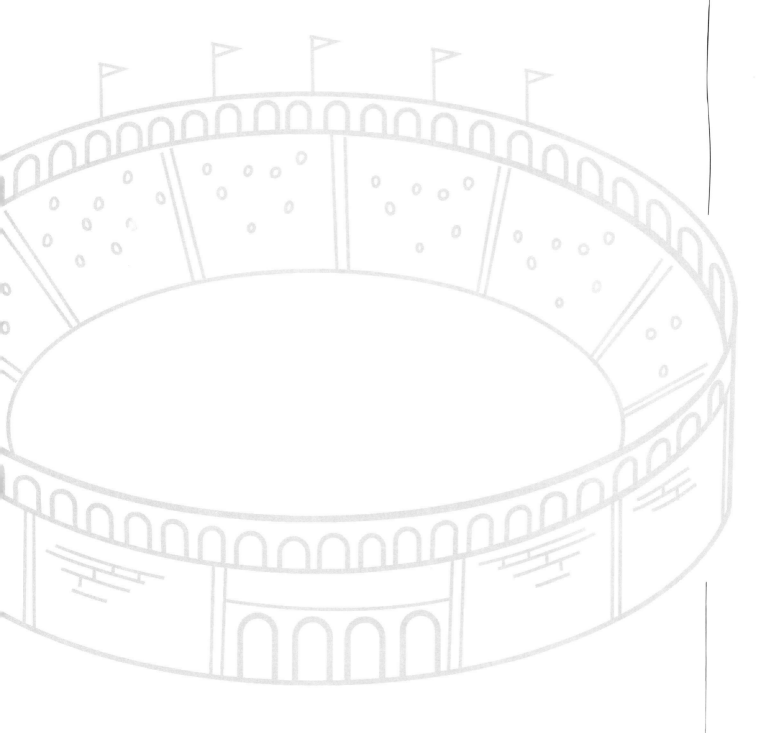

ATTACK OF THE KILLER . . .

What's tearing up this town?

Doodlemaster

MAD SCIENCE

Draw yourself as a mad scientist in your secret laboratory.

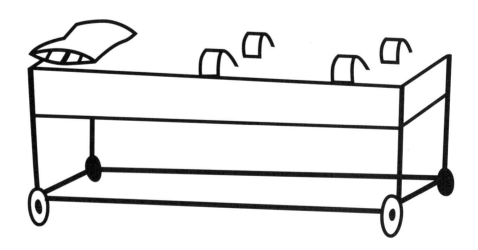

What's growing in that pietri dish?

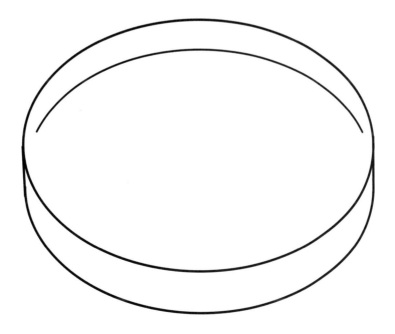

SUPER CHALLENGE

You have a cardboard box, a roll of duct tape,
and a pair of scissors. Make something!
Draw your invention here:

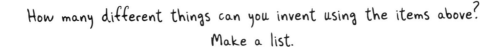

How many different things can you invent using the items above?
Make a list.

CHEF DOODLEMASTER

You're a chef in a restaurant just for kids. Invent and draw the following:

A new flavor for potato chips.

The ultimate pizza.

The best dessert ever.

A super junk food.

WOULD YOU RATHER EAT:

Carrots or celery?

Broccoli or brussels sprout?

Chicken fingers or grilled cheese?

Liver or raw fish?

Granola bar or candy bar?

Pizza or a hot dog?

Waffles or pancakes?

Bacon or bologna?

Apples or bananas?

Ice cream or frozen yogurt?

FUNNY FACES

Draw your facial expressions:

You've just been told that dinner is brussels sprout, split pea soup, and broccoli (minus the cheese sauce).

You've just found out you're going to star in the next big action movie!

You just won a million dollars!

You just accepted a dare to eat a new dish in the cafeteria called "spinach surprise."

Doodlemaster

Your favorite band is going
to play at your school!

You shut off your alarm and
went back to sleep and now
you're late for school...AGAIN!

You have to clean
your room—all of it!

You accidentally broke
a neighbor's window
while playing ball.

FAME, FORTUNE, AND BESTSELLERS

You're a famous rocker and your autobiography is a bestseller.
Draw your book cover here:

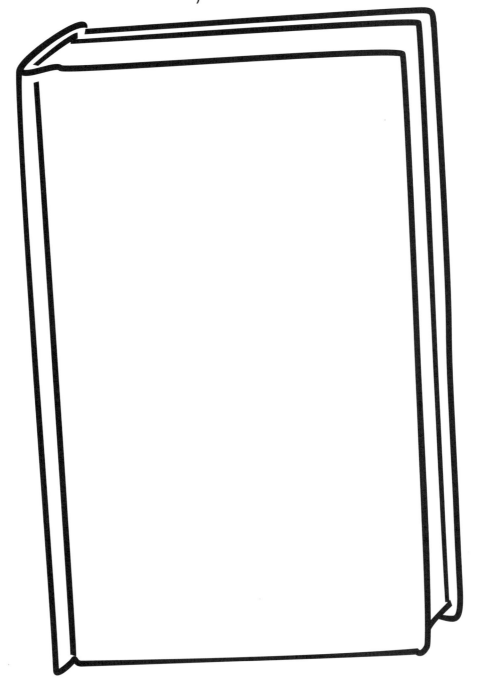

Write a description of your book here:

Write a quote from your best review:

BUILD YOUR TROPHY ROOM

Design a room to hold the dozens of trophies you've won.

Now draw your biggest and best trophy.
What did you win it for?

GARAGE BAND

Turn your garage into the best practice space ever:

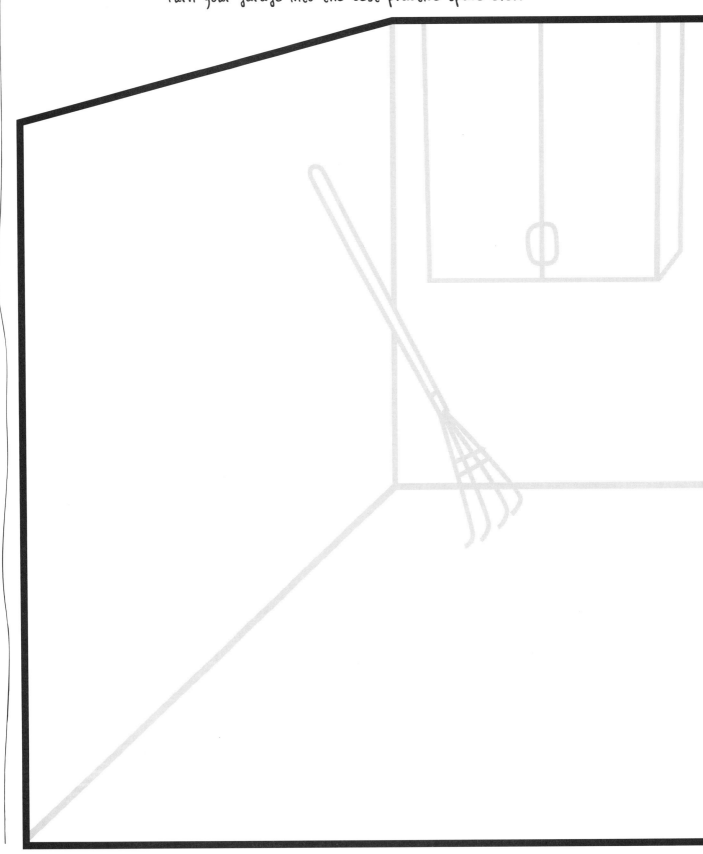

Doodlemaster

PERSONALIZE YOUR TOUR BUS

Draw the outside of your tour bus.

What are its coolest features?

Doodlemaster

Now, show off what's on the inside.
Is it comfy, expensive, luxurious, and full of gadgets,
or dirty, rugged, and cool?

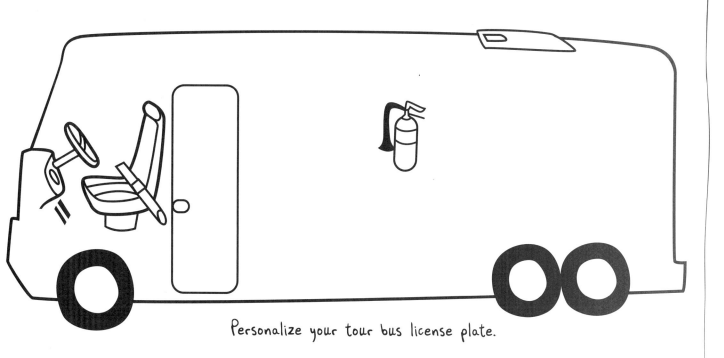

Personalize your tour bus license plate.

SPACE OUT!

Draw the planet you'd most like to travel to.
What will you find there? Don't forget to add your stellar spaceship!

Doodlemaster

MONSTER MESS

What gave this monster bad breath?

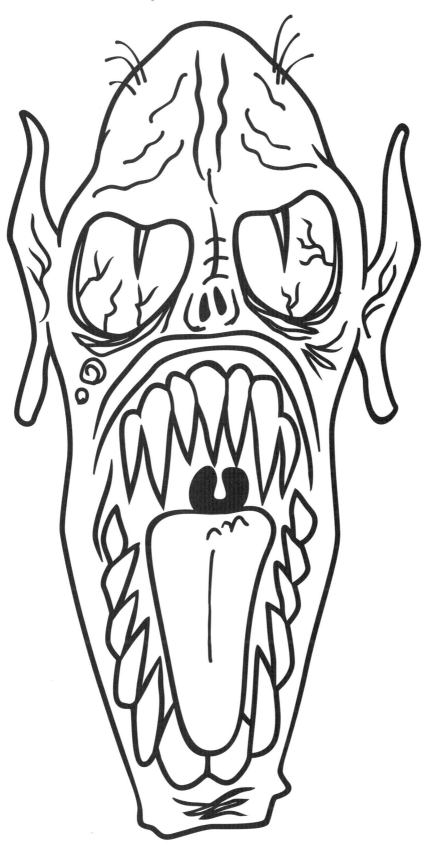

SPECIAL EFFECTS

Turn these faces into the following movie characters:

Spy

Old person

Vampire

Zombie

Doodlemaster

Spaceship captain

Evil genius

Alien

Superhero

What's your favorite special effect ever in a movie?

CALLING ALL DOODLEMASTERS

Here's your chance to invent the coolest cell phone ever.
What does it do?

GET THE BAND TO THE CONCERT

DESIGN YOUR RIDE

Now that you are a rock star, you can afford the most awesome bike ever built.
Draw your dream bike here.

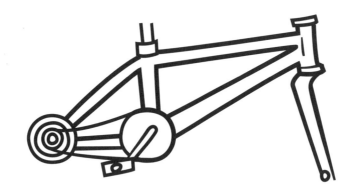

Doodlemaster

You KNOW you have to wear a helmet—so make it cool!

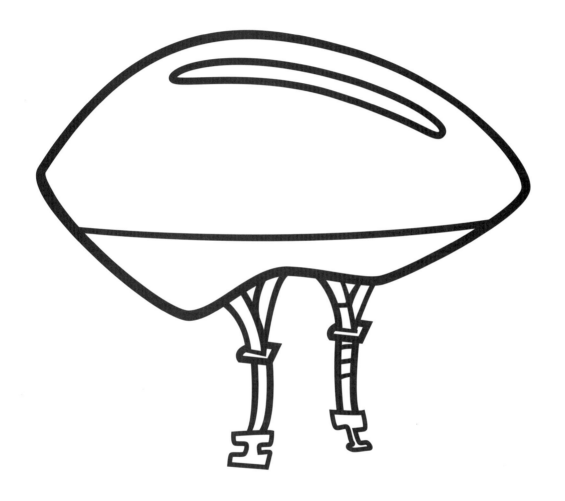

SKATEBOARD PARK

What's going on in the skaters' park today?

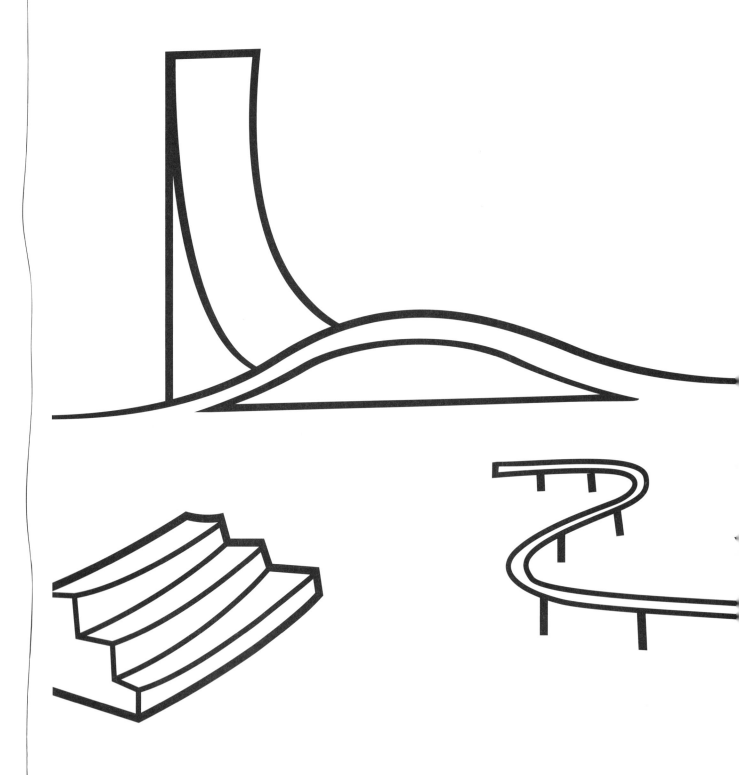

Doodlemaster

Don't forget to decorate
your skateboard.

FAMILY BONDING

Draw a picture of your family. Then, turn them all into aliens—including you!

THE ULTIMATE RESTAURANT!

Design your own restaurant menu with anything you want to eat. Don't forget appetizers, dinner, and desserts! Maybe there's a whole separate category for junk food. Go ahead and draw some of the grossest items on the menu.

Top three name ideas for your restaurant:

1.

2.

3.

Top three favorite foods:

1.

2.

3.

DRESS CODE

Personalize your hoodie!

Now, personalize your sneakers...

...and your cap!

WHAT'S IN THIS BOX?

WISH LIST

BE CAREFUL WHAT YOU WISH FOR!

List and then draw your top three wishes of all time.

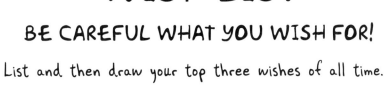

PORTAL TO ANOTHER WORLD

Hmmmm...maybe you shouldn't have opened that
portal to another world, but since you did...

What does it look like?

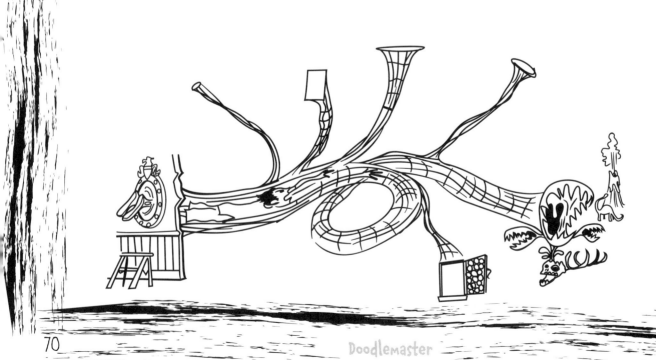

Doodlemaster

What lives there?

Does time work the same way it does here? Faster? Slower? By how much?

List as many details about your new world as possible.

CREATURE FEATURE

Create the most horrible creature imaginable for the next blockbuster monster movie!

Doodlemaster

What is its name?

How big is it?

Where does it live?

What is the scariest thing about it?

Now draw what it's doing in its big scene.

YOU'RE THE DJ!

You're in charge of the music for a major event.
Draw yourself as the DJ, and don't forget your equipment!

My favorite style of music is:

My top 3 favorite bands:
1.
2.
3.

My top 3 favorite solo performers:
1.
2.
3.

My top 3 favorite music videos:
1.
2.
3.

My top 3 favorite albums:
1.
2.
3.

My top 3 favorite songs:
1.
2.
3.

My favorite songs for:

• Chilling out:

• Feeling energetic:

• Playing air guitar:

• Playing air drums:

• Listening to in the car:

• Falling asleep:

MUSICMASTER

Draw a scene from your music video!

Personalize your electric guitar.

SPREAD THE WORD

Make a concert poster for your band's big show!

Doodlemaster

WICKED FUN

Draw yourself as a supervillain.

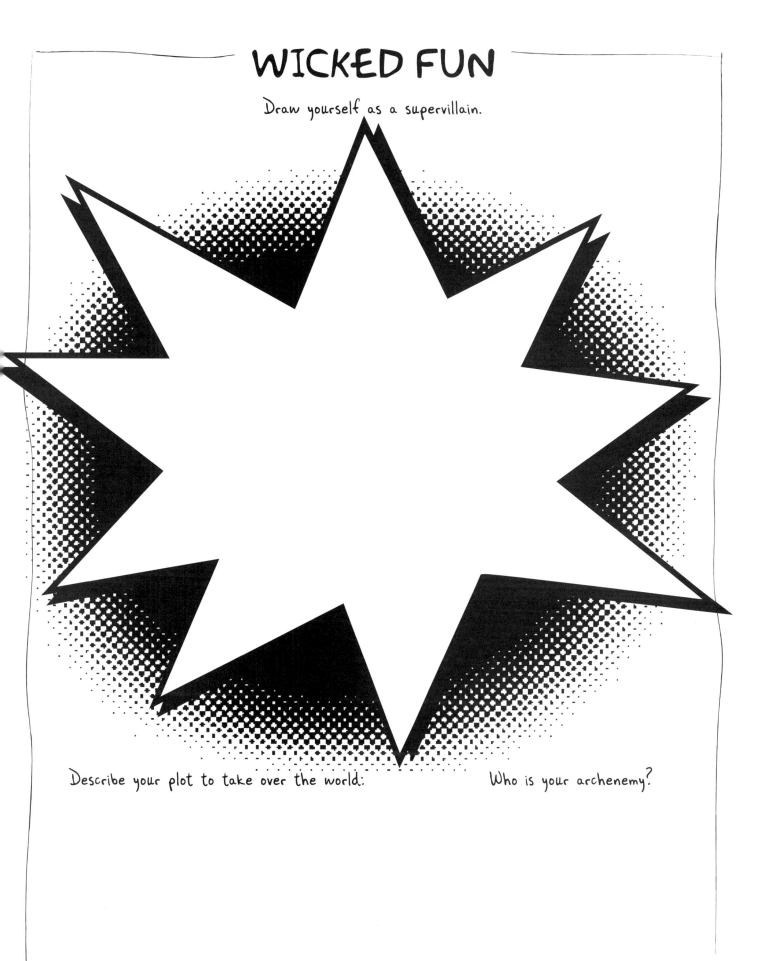

Describe your plot to take over the world:

Who is your archenemy?

YUCK!

Uh-oh. You fell into a sewer grate.
What's down there with you?

Doodlemaster

VIDEO GAME DESIGNER

Nice work landing that gig designing video games!

Draw the main character
in your game.

Now, design the big beast your
hero has to fight to win the game.

List as many details as you can about your new game.

BRIDGE THE GAP!

Build the bridge that will get the band to the concert.

Doodlemaster

ROCK N' ROLLER COASTER!

Design the ultimate roller coaster, using whatever theme you want.

TOY STORY

Design a toy. It can be for you, your little brother/sister, or even your pet!

What is your toy called?

Where will you advertise it?

How much will it cost?

What is the slogan for your big ad campaign?

Doodlemaster

CLOWN CAR

Road trip! How many clowns can you draw in this car?

CATCH A WAVE!

Draw yourself surfing the most awesome wave ever.
Don't forget to design your surfboard.

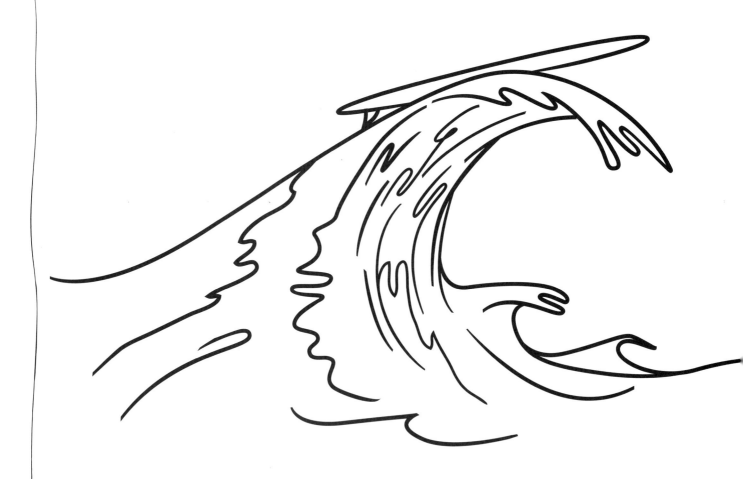

Doodlemaster

Whoa! Is that a shark fin? Describe how you'll get to shore safely:

STOP THAT DINO!

Build something to stop this dinosaur in its tracks!

Doodlemaster

WHAT'S AT THE TOP OF THIS LADDER?

COMEDY CLUB

You're the headline act in a comedy club. It's up to you to make 'em laugh!
Draw yourself on the stage.

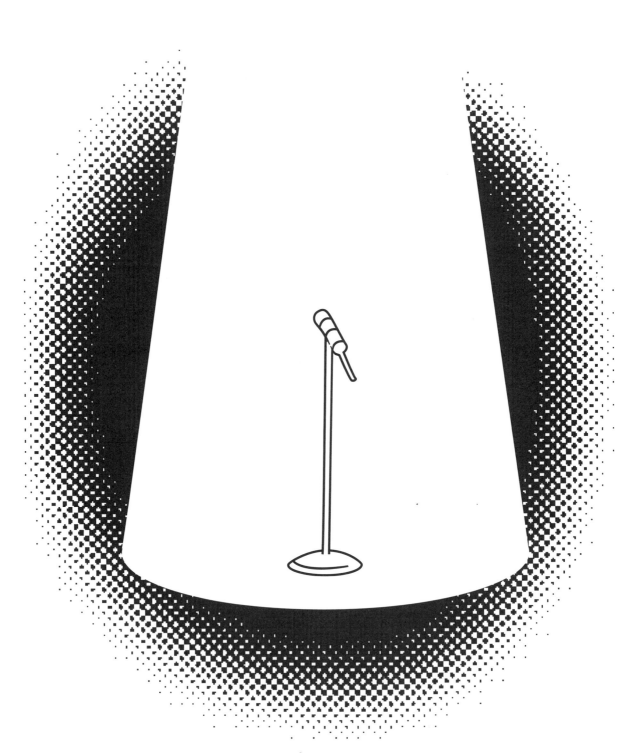

Doodlemaster

My favorite joke is:

My favorite comedians from movies or TV are:

My favorite funny movies and TV shows:

My favorite funny books are:

Why are these kids laughing? Draw it!

BA HA HA HA

SNACK ATTACK!

Draw yourself being attacked by your favorite food.

WORLD TOUR

Where have you been? Where do you want to go? Mark the stops on your world tour with an X. Mark the places you've already been with a ★.

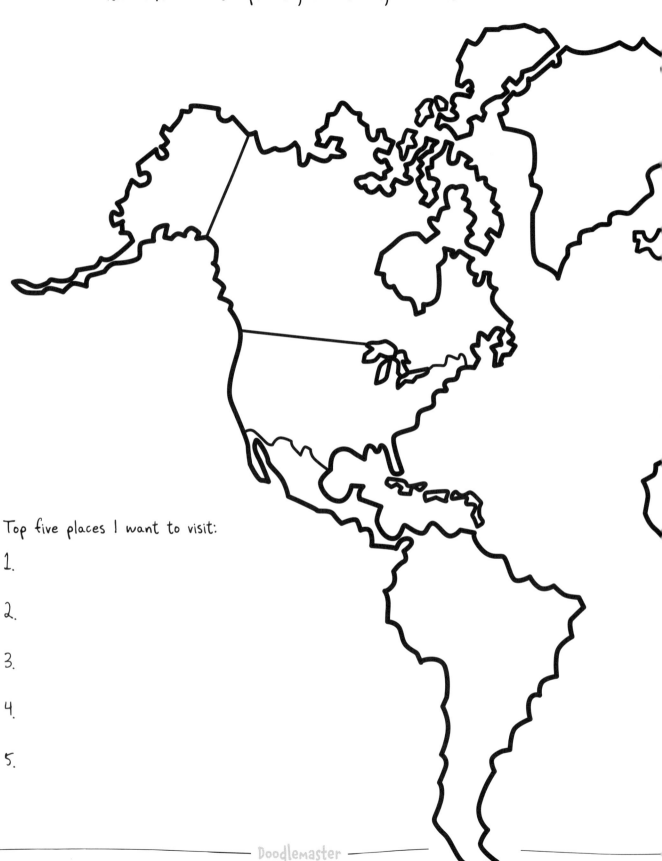

Top five places I want to visit:

1.

2.

3.

4.

5.

Doodlemaster

If I could go on vacation anywhere RIGHT NOW, it would be:

Best vacation I've ever been on:

One place I never want to go back to and why:

WANTED!

Draw yourself as an outlaw and be sure to write on this poster what you're wanted for!

Doodlemaster

ROBOKID

Draw yourself as a robot.

What is your coolest function?

Doodlemaster

SUPERSIZE ME!

Draw yourself superstrong.

What is the heaviest thing you can lift?
Draw it here!

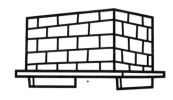

ROCK OUT!

Trace the images below and use them to create your own rock band logo, skateboard decorations, guitar-case labels, or notebook art.

Doodlemaster

JUMP AHEAD

Draw yourself in five years.

How old will you be?

What grade will you be in?

How tall will you be?

What will be your favorite:

- Food?

- Sport?

- Type of music?

- Subject in school?

What are the top 3 coolest things you'll do between now and then?

1.

2.

3.

Name one thing you promise NOT to do between now and then.

Doodlemaster

WHAT ATE THIS?!

YOU'RE BOOKED!

You're the author of a bestselling book about
being a famous rock star. Who is your book dedicated to?
Design your dedication page below:

Uh-oh!
What's hiding
under
this book?

Doodlemaster

WOULD YOU RATHER...?

CIRCLE YOUR CHOICE:

Scratch a blackboard or listen to someone scratching a blackboard?

Play piano or play guitar?

Have X-ray vision or night vision?

Meet a real spy or meet a pro football player?

Give up candy for a year or eat a new vegetable every day for a month?

Kiss a snake or kiss a goldfish?

Have a driver's license or have a pilot's license?

Never dream again or give up your sense of smell?

Wear the same pair of pants to school for an entire month or
sing "The Star Spangled Banner" in front of the whole school?

Not sleep for two whole days or not eat anything for two whole days?

Smell like flowers or B.O.?

Get chased by a bully or a German shepherd?

Dress up like a giant milk shake and give out fliers in front of a
fast-food restaurant for money or eat someone else's booger for free?

Hold a live piranha or kiss a teacher?

Spread mashed-up earthworms on your toast or recite a poem in front of the class?

Wear a pirate eye patch to school for a whole month
or wear only the color pink to school for two weeks?

Have a billion dollars or never get sick again?

Be so famous your name was on TV and in textbooks
or make contact with alien life-forms?

Never have to clean your room again or
never have to do homework again?

Help your dad clean the house or
help your mom mow the lawn?

SPEAKER BLOWOUT

Uh-oh! The new speakers in my room are SO loud!
Draw what happens when you crank them up to top volume.

Doodlemaster

GROSSER THAN GROSS

WHAT'S NASTIER?

(Circle your pick.)

Farting or burping?

Blisters or zits?

Broccoli or brussels sprout?

Roaches or lice?

Doggy doo or baby poo?

Your socks after gym class or
your lunch left in your locker too long?

Falling in mud or falling in garbage?

Mice or maggots?

Hairy toes or hairy knuckles?

Dog gas or dad gas?

Boogers or scabs?

RANKING THE RANK

Number these ten things in order from most foul to least foul. Then, compare the results with your friends. How alike are you?

Farts_____

Burps_____

Boogers_____

Scabs_____

Eye crust_____

Dirty underwear_____

Smelly feet_____

Barf _____

Vegetables_____

Girls_____

Draw the grossest thing you can think of here:

DON'T LET THE BEDBUGS BITE!

The best dream I ever had:

My worst nightmare:

One dream I keep having
over and over again:

When I'm stressed, I dream that:

Now, go back and doodle images from your dreams all over this page!

Doodlemaster

WHAT IF?

If I could fly, I'd...

If I were invisible, I'd...

If I were super-small, I'd...

If I could shoot fire out of my hands, I'd...

WHAT THE WORLD NEEDS TO KNOW ABOUT ME

Hair color:

Eye color:

How tall?

Nicknames:

Nicknames that make me cringe:

Number of people who live in my house:

Star sign:

Own room or share a room?

Brothers and sisters?

Best subject:

Worst subject:

Pets?

Favorite instrument:

Favorite TV show:

Favorite TV show theme song:

Favorite character on a TV show:

Favorite movie:

Favorite movie trilogy:

Favorite kind of movie (action, comedy, drama, animated, foreign, romance, documentary):

Favorite actor or actress:

Favorite character in a movie:

Favorite cartoon:

Favorite video game:

Favorite video game system:

Favorite thing to do on my computer:

Favorite hobby:

Favorite place to hang out:

Favorite thing to do right after school:

Does the word "favorite" look funny to you right about now?

Favorite thing to do on a rainy day:

Least favorite thing to do on a rainy day:

Favorite sport:

Favorite sports team:

Favorite Olympic sport:

Favorite kind of potato chip:

Favorite flavor of ice cream:

Favorite kind of soda:

Favorite color:

Favorite childhood memory:

Favorite item of clothing:

Favorite room in my house:

Favorite place to be alone:

Favorite place to bike to:

Favorite quote:

Favorite book:

Favorite author:

Favorite magazine, comic book, or newspaper:

Favorite word or phrase to say over and over and over again:

Favorite sound:

Favorite time of year:

Favorite time of day:

Favorite month:

Favorite charitable cause I'm really into:

Favorite toy or action figure:

Favorite thing to do when no one is looking:

Favorite thing about Saturday:

Favorite thing about Tuesday:

Favorite number:

FILL IN THE BLANKS

_____ is mean. _____ is meaner. _____ is the meanest.

_____ is cool. _____ is cooler. _____ is the coolest.

_____ is boring. _____ is even more boring.

_____ is a total snoozefest.

If I could switch places with anyone in the world for a day, it would be:_____

If I could share an order of fries with anyone in the world—living or dead—it would be:

_____

If I could be famous for doing any one thing, it would be:_____

If I could make a guest appearance on any TV show, it would be:_____

The TV show I secretly love but will never admit to watching is:_____

FOR EACH OF THE FOLLOWING, CHECK ONE:

Do you know what you want
to be when you grow up?　　　　　❏ SURE　❏ KINDA　❏ NOT IN A MILLION YEARS

Would you ever sing in a school musical?　❏ SURE　❏ KINDA　❏ NOT IN A MILLION YEARS

Would you ever act in a class play?　　❏ SURE　❏ KINDA　❏ NOT IN A MILLION YEARS

Would you ever run for student
government president?　　　　　❏ SURE　❏ KINDA　❏ NOT IN A MILLION YEARS

Would you ever try out for the
football team?　　　　　　　❏ SURE　❏ KINDA　❏ NOT IN A MILLION YEARS

Would you ever join the chess club?　❏ SURE　❏ KINDA　❏ NOT IN A MILLION YEARS

Would you ever join a book club?　　❏ SURE　❏ KINDA　❏ NOT IN A MILLION YEARS

Would you ever run a marathon
(that's 26 miles!)?   ❑ SURE   ❑ KINDA   ❑ NOT IN A MILLION YEARS

Would you ever eat a bug for money?   ❑ SURE   ❑ KINDA   ❑ NOT IN A MILLION YEARS

Would you ever tell on your best friend
(if the situation made it necessary)?   ❑ SURE   ❑ KINDA   ❑ NOT IN A MILLION YEARS

Would you ever take something
that didn't belong to you?   ❑ SURE   ❑ KINDA   ❑ NOT IN A MILLION YEARS

Would you ever borrow something
without asking?   ❑ SURE   ❑ KINDA   ❑ NOT IN A MILLION YEARS

Would you ever sleep in footie pajamas?   ❑ SURE   ❑ KINDA   ❑ NOT IN A MILLION YEARS

Would you ever let your mom hug
you in front of your friends?   ❑ SURE   ❑ KINDA   ❑ NOT IN A MILLION YEARS

Would you ever ride your bike
without telling your parents where
you were going?   ❑ SURE   ❑ KINDA   ❑ NOT IN A MILLION YEARS

UH-OH! LATE FOR THE CONCERT AGAIN!

How will you get there?

Doodlemaster

BRAND-NEW BEDROOM

If I could give my bedroom an extreme makeover, it would look like this:

If there was a fire in my bedroom the top five things I'd save are:

If there was a secret compartment in my closet, I'd keep this stuff in there:

MY MILLIONAIRE MANSION

Rock stars don't live in ordinary houses. Draw your dream house here.

Doodlemaster

DRAW YOUR HAPPY PLACE!

Now, put yourself in it.

KUNG FU KICKOFF!

Draw a samurai battle between any two people, animals, or imaginary creatures you choose. Where does it happen? Who wins? It's up to you. Be creative!

THE MOVIE OF YOUR LIFE

What actor would play you in the movie of your life?_____

Your mom?_____

Dad?_____

Siblings?_____

Friends?_____

Would it be a comedy, drama, tragedy, horror movie, or artsy hit?_____

The opening scene would take place:_____

The soundtrack would include songs like:_____

The director would be:_____

Storyboard a scene from the movie of your life here.

RATE THIS!

What's your take? Draw an arrow to rank these activities/things on a scale from **SUPER-LAME** to **SUPERCOOL**.

SKATEBOARDING

PLAYING DRUMS

HIP-HOP DANCING

KARAOKE

READING

HOMEWORK

DRAWING

PAINTBALL

TONIGHT'S DINNER

BUILDING THINGS

SCHOOL

WATCHING DVDS

PLAYING GUITAR

BLOGGING

Doodlemaster

MONSTER-MAKING

CHESS

SCRABBLE

CHORES

DRESSING UP FOR HALLOWEEN

DRESSING UP FOR CLASS PHOTOS

BASEBALL

FOOTBALL

SWORD FIGHTS

KUNG FU

GETTING CALLED ON IN CLASS

ROBOTS

HORROR MOVIES

SCI-FI MOVIES

GOING TO THE LIBRARY

SHOPPING

CREATE YOUR OWN CARTOON!

Draw your own cartoon character. Then draw its best friend and the world they live in.

CRASH COURSE! Now, draw what happens when a cow falls out of the sky!

Doodlemaster

ROCKIN' WEB PAGE

Draw your band's homepage.

Design the logo for your band here.

Now, invent your own Web show. What's it about? Who does it star? When is it on? Does it include music, jokes, or stories? Do you have guest stars? Think of as many details about your show as you can and list them here.

TRAPPED!

You are trapped on a desert island for a whole month.
You can only bring five things with you. Draw them here.

What kind of shelter will you build? What is it made of?
Draw it here.

Now, draw your escape plan. How do you get off the island?

Doodlemaster

INCOGNITO

Draw yourself in disguise.
What do you see?

SUPERSTAR!

Draw anything you want.
It's your book!

Doodlemaster